No More Nightmares

Biljana Trakilovic

tellwell

Tellwell Talent
www.tellwell.ca

ISBN
978-0-2288-5377-0 (Hardcover)
978-0-2288-4385-6 (Paperback)

Sometimes when I sleep, I would have a nightmare. They seem so real. I would see monsters and all other scary things. Even my dinosaurs seem to come alive and sometimes I feel like my room spins and I would wake up crying.

Mum told me not to be afraid. I 'am still little and nightmares seem to be real, they are just part of my growing and they will soon disappear. She would read me a book and snuggle me until I fall back to sleep.

Mum and dad made me a new room, it is small and cozy. My fairy lights are on all night to make me feel comfortable and safe. It seems like I don't have as many nightmares in my new room, but sometimes I do.

I love my new room it is small and cozy, surrounded with all of my favorite toys. I spend much more play time in my room. It is just the way I like it, fun, small but still plenty of room for me to play, jump and even ride on my little horse Blake.

Mum gave me a new bunny, which is small white and fluffy, with pink feet and long ears. I sleep with him at night and nightmares seem to disappear. I have lots of soft toys, but this one is special to me, it makes me feel warm and safe when he is with me.

Seems like my pink feet bunny and my fairy lights, have scared my nightmares away, or maybe they just don't like my new room, it doesn't have as many scary toys around. I'm not sure but it works for me.

In the morning when I wake up, I don't remember much of what my nightmare was about, only some scary toys that made me cry and stories that mum told me so I can go back to sleep. That is the good part, as my mornings are always playful and happy with my little brother, so I don't mind not remembering my whole dream that I had during the night.

Mum still reads me a book at night, now to me and my pink feet bunny, we fall asleep with the softness in her voice and have funny and sweet dreams.

The end.

Milton Keynes UK
Ingram Content Group UK Ltd.
UKHW052208060224
437338UK00002B/7

9 780228 843856